THIS BOOK BELONGS TO

9 781652 360698